Nick's Guitar Gym:

Triads and Triad Scales, Vol. 1

Strings 1, 2, and 3

By Nick Rawson

Table of Contents

About the Author	p. 3
Triads for Strings 1,2, and 3	p. 4
Theory	p. 6
Triad Cheat Sheet	p. 7
Major & Minor Keys	p. 8
Triad Scales	p. 20
Neckology	p. 32
6 String Triad Scales	p. 34
All 27 Triad Inversions	p. 39

About the Author

I played some guitar as a little kid. Took a lesson when I was six.

They said, "Don't bring him back."

Took another lesson in high school—the guy was boring. But by then, I was playing every day and pretty much every day since.

I was a music major in college, then joined a rock musical called *Stomp*, in which I acted, played guitar, and sang and wrote songs. The show was produced by Joseph Papp and played Off-Broadway in New York for eight months before touring throughout Europe and playing in Paris, London, Amsterdam, Munich, Berlin, and many more.

That was fun.

But once I started teaching, I discovered that it was my calling.

I taught in Austin, Texas at Austin City Music for ten years, then moved to Houston and taught at Rockin' Robin for about another ten years. Now I teach private lessons in Montrose.

Besides teaching, I have played in a classic rock band called The deadBeats and an acoustic group called The Aficionados. If you're in Houston, you can find me playing original tunes at EQ Heights on the second Saturday of every month—I'd love to see you sometime.

Now, let's have some fun with that guitar.

Triads For Strings 1, 2, & 3

In music, a **triad** is a group of three notes in thirds, stacked on top of one another. You have the root, a third, and a fifth—but not always in that order.

In this book, you will learn how to *use triads to play scales.* Or, as a guitar player would say, you will learn how to *use chords to play lead.* By learning a few major, minor, and 7th melody-chords, we can combine them to have a *customized scale* for each chord throughout the chord progression of a song, with chord tones and passing tones clearly displayed so you can resolve up or down and travel throughout the neck of the guitar.

Jimi Hendrix was a master of this. If you listen to his music, you can hear him following the chord progression with his melodies.

Use this book of *Triads and Triad Scales* if you want to have fun right away playing shapes— every exercise in this book can be played using just nine shapes. You do not need to read notes, but you will need to read some tablature, or tab, to know which fret to play. You will also need to know that the 12 notes always come in this order:

E – F – F♯ – G – G♯ – A – B♭ – B – C – C♯ – D – D♯

This Book will employ these 9 shapes:

The 3 Major Shapes

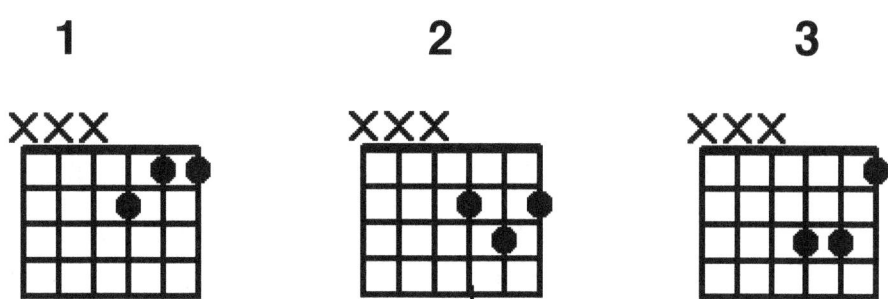

The 3 Minor Shapes

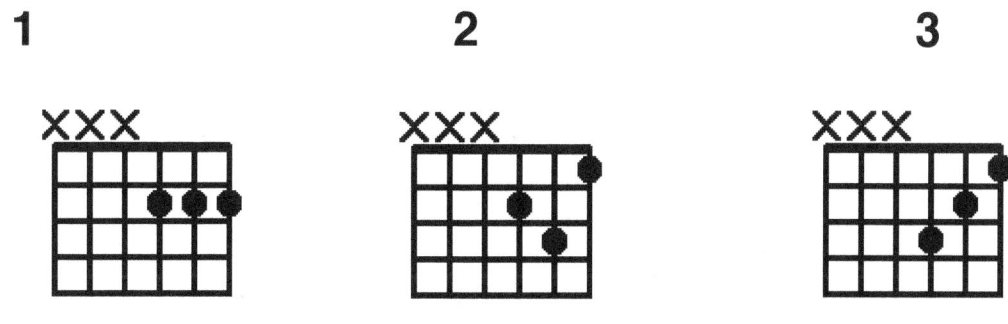

The 3 Dominant 7th Shapes

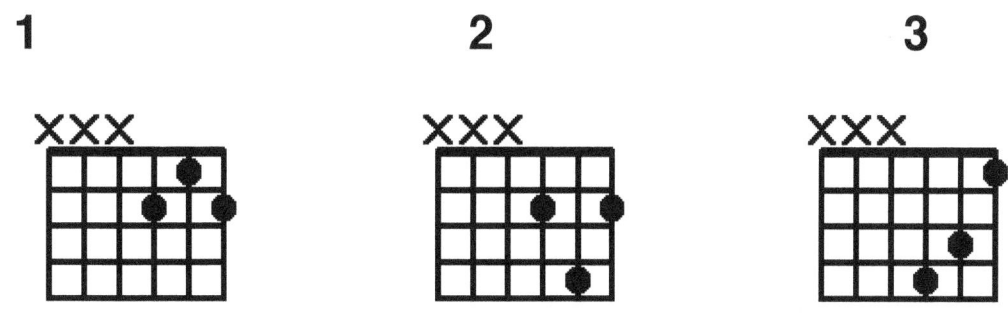

Theory

I don't want to put you to sleep by going on and on about musical theory, but I will say this: To be a better guitar player, you want and need to know some of the basics.

Think of it this way—you know the letters of the alphabet, even if you've never come across a particular word before, right? That knowledge can help you pronounce that word—and your knowledge of other, similar words can sometimes even help you figure out what it means. Music is the same way. Once you learn the basics of the *system*, you're well-equipped to deal with things you haven't necessarily seen before. That's good news! It means you don't have to memorize everything. But you do need to know a few things—like the alphabet.

The next page contains the basics of the system. If you know them, you are in the game. If you don't know them, you're just guessing. There are some brilliant people and some good guessers out there. But I needed all the help I could get when I was figuring out the basics of music. With them, though, I'm in the game.

Let's take a look at:
- The chromatic scale (all 12 notes in order)
- The cycle of 4ths
- The major triads
- Triad formulas

Nick's Guitar Gym

TRIAD CHEAT-SHEET

1	2	3	4	5	6
Every	**B**ody	**G**ets	**D**own	**A**t	**E**d's

Major Triads

Root - Third - Fifth

C - E - G
F - A - C
C - E - G
Bb - D - F
Eb - G - Bb
Ab - C - Eb
Db - F - Ab
Gb - Bb - Db
F# - A# - C#
B - D# - F#
E - G# - D
A - C# - E
D - F# - A
G - B - D

\# = Sharp; b = Flat

Triad Formulas

Major   1 - 3 - 5

Minor   1 - b3 - 5

Augmented+ 1 - 3 - #5

Diminished° 1 - b3 - b5

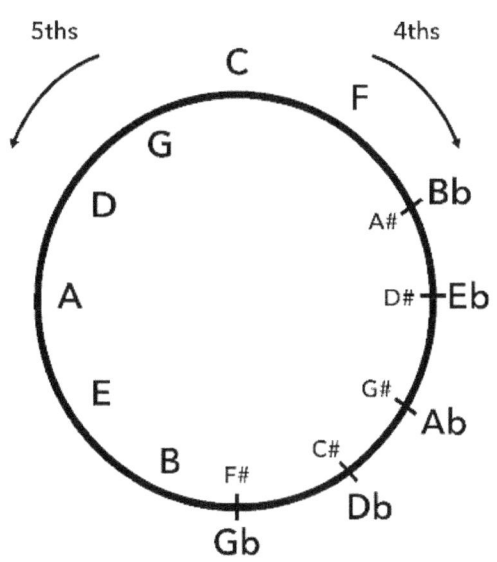

E - F - F# - G - G# - A - Bb - B - C - C# - D - D#

Major and Minor Keys

The following page lists all of the major and minor scales and chords, and all the major and minor keys. It is the matrix for **tertian harmony**, which is the harmonic system of notes and chords built on thirds. It can be used as a reference.

Nick's Guitar Gym: Triads and Triad Scales, Vol. 1: Strings 1, 2, and 3

I	ii	iii	IV	V	vi	vii
MAJOR	minor	minor	MAJOR	MAJOR	minor	diminished
III	iv	v	vi	VII	i	ii
C	D	E	F	G	A	B
G	A	B	C	D	E	F#
D	E	F#	G	A	B	C#
A	B	C#	D	E	F#	G#
E	F#	G#	A	B	C#	D#
B	C#	D#	E	F#	G#	A#
F#	G#	A#	B	C#	D#	E#
C#	D#	E#	F#	G#	A#	B#
F	G	A	Bb	C	D	E
Bb	C	D	Eb	F	G	A
Eb	F	G	Ab	Bb	C	D
Ab	Bb	C	Db	Eb	F	G
Db	Eb	F	Gb	Ab	Bb	C
Gb	Ab	Bb	Cb	Db	Eb	F
Cb	Db	Eb	Fb	Gb	Ab	Bb

NICK RAWSON

Download-Install-Practice-Apply

One reason I try to leave text at a minimum is that the exercises in these books are like pushups—you benefit from doing them, whether you understand the theory behind them or not. You will come to understand these exercises eventually, through playing them. The way I look at it, you can either "learn to play," or you can "play to learn." Playing to learn is more fun.

So this book is not necessarily about explaining triads. Rather, it is a compendium of the information you will be asked for by any song or jam session, and you will gain insight as you go along. It's more about exercises that guitarists should practice. Think of it as software that is downloaded and installed by repetition!

Every song has a chord progression that guides the player along. These are the chords you will be asked for. You want to know what the chord progression is asking you for and you want to be able to find it, and quickly... all of it!

Major Shape Chords, Strings 123 as G Major

Hint: The lowest number on the tab will be the index finger

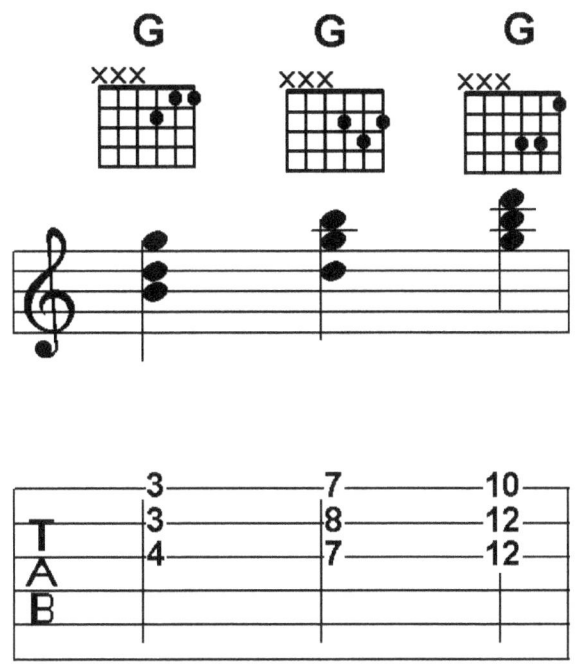

Major Shape Arpeggios, Strings 123 as G Major

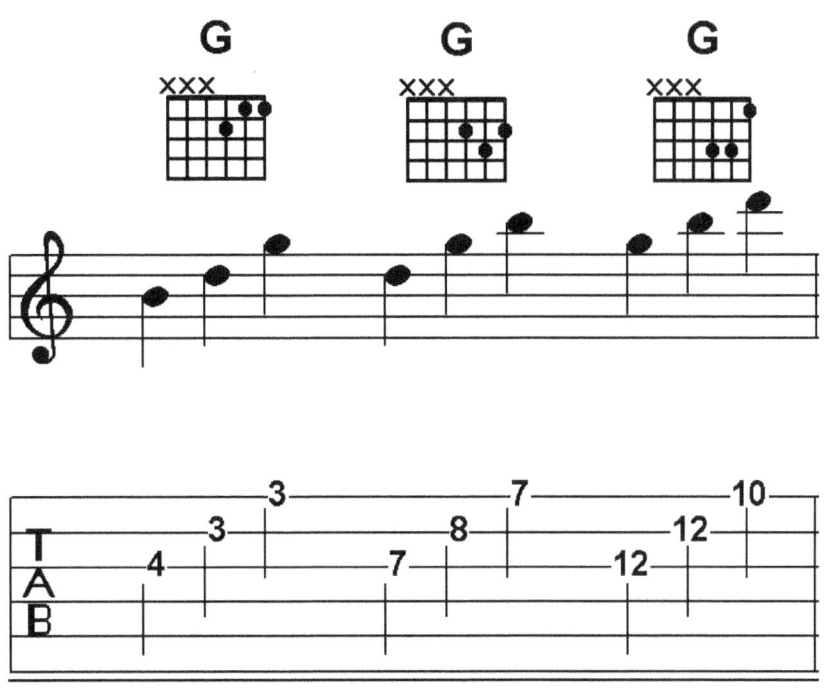

Minor Shape Chords, Strings 123 as G Minor

Hint: The lowest number on the tab will be the index finger

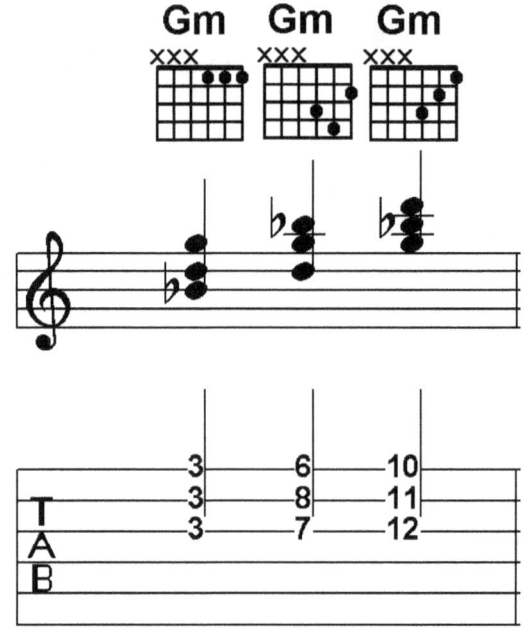

Minor Shape Arpeggios, Strings 123 as G Minor

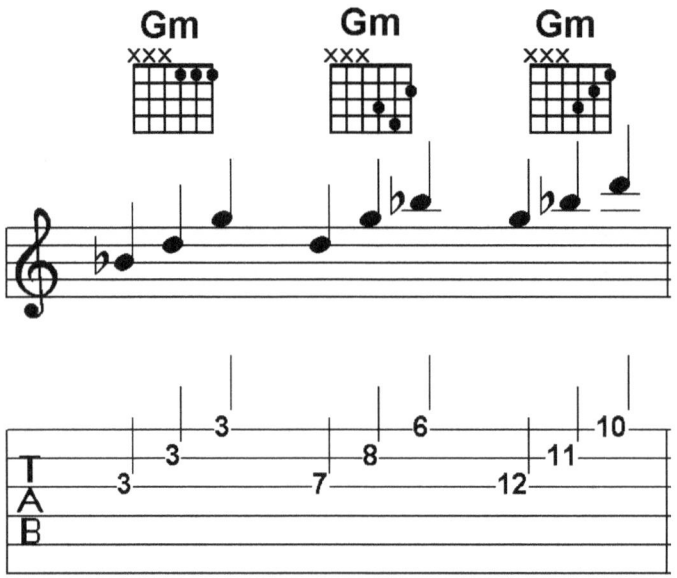

7th Shape Chords, Strings 123 as D7th

Hint: The lowest number on the tab will be the index finger

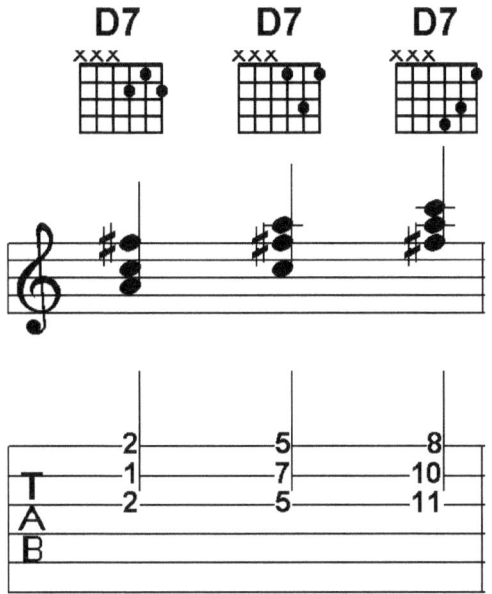

7th Shape Arpeggios, Strings 123 as D7th

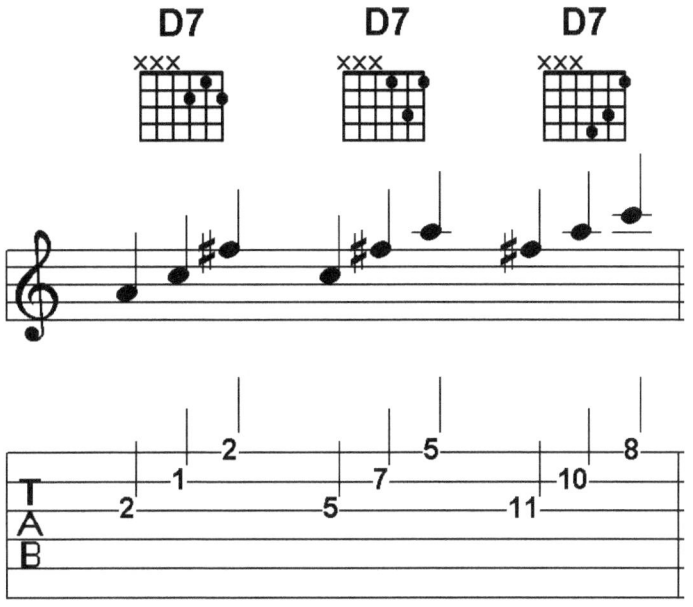

Triads

Triads are chords. All chords are made from triads.

Here are all the major chords in the key of G on strings 1, 2, and 3. The root is in the melody (in this case, string 1).

Major Key Linear, Strings 123, Root on String 1

Key of G Major

We will use just these 3 shapes with the root on string 1

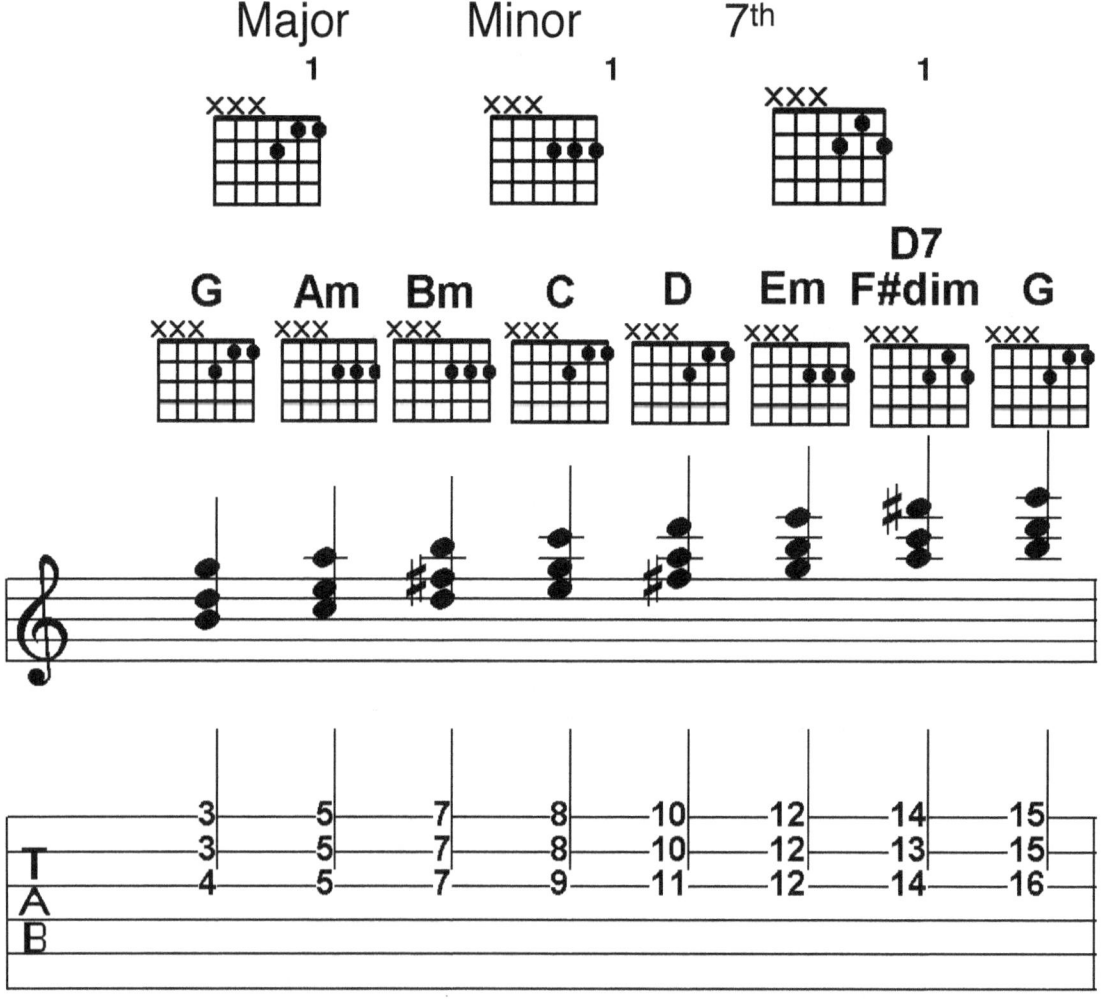

Hint: The lowest number on the tab will be the index finger

Major Key Linear, Strings 123, Root on String 2

Key of D Major

We will use just these 3 shapes with the root on string 2

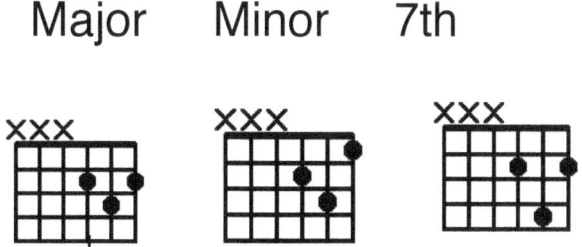

Major   Minor   7th

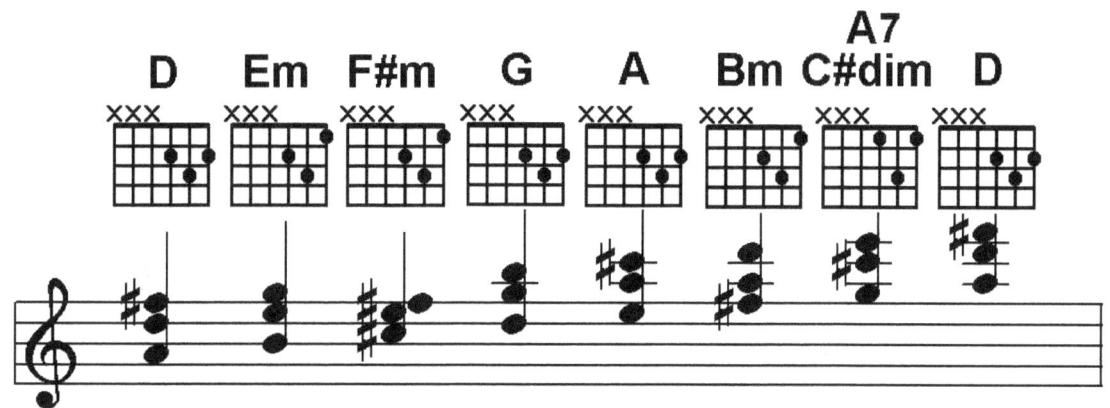

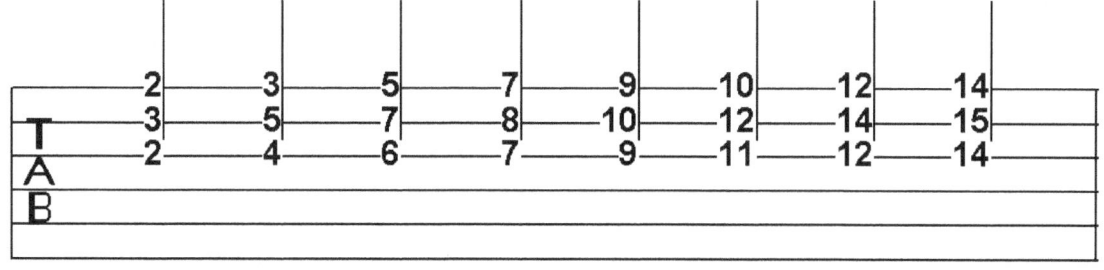

Hint: The lowest number on the tab will be the index finger

Major key linear 123 Root on String 3

Key of C Major

We will use just these 3 shapes with the root on string 3

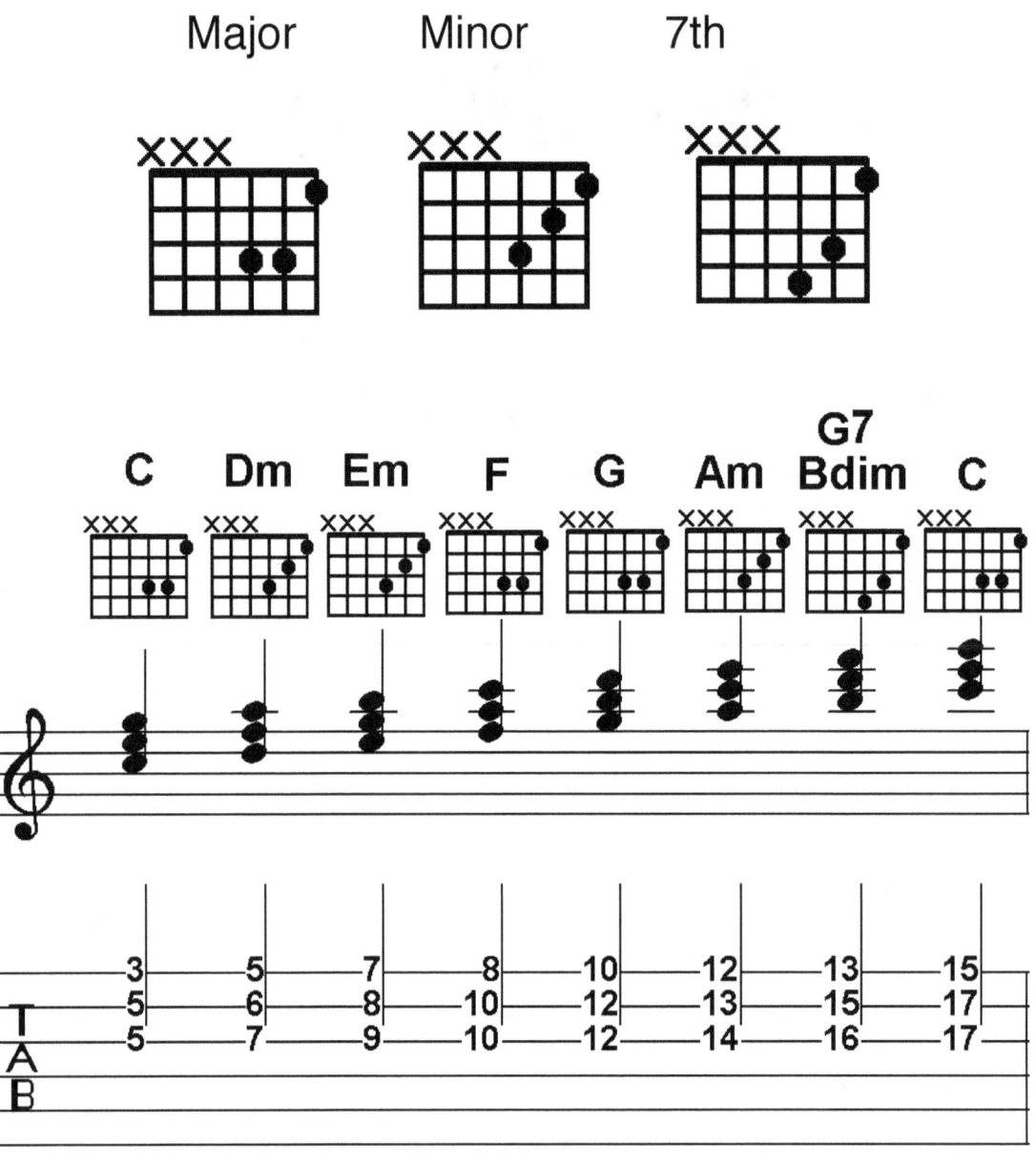

Hint: The lowest number on the tab will be the index finger

Minor Key Linear, Strings 123, Root on String 1

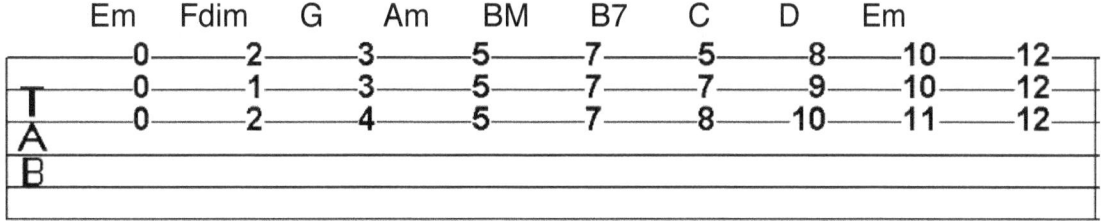

Minor Key Linear, Strings 123, Root on String 2

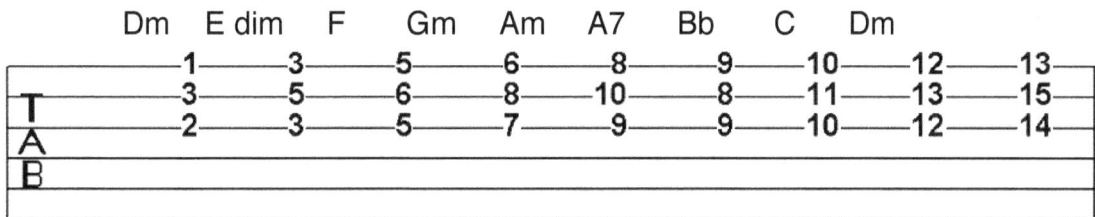

Minor Key Linear, Strings 123, Root on String 3

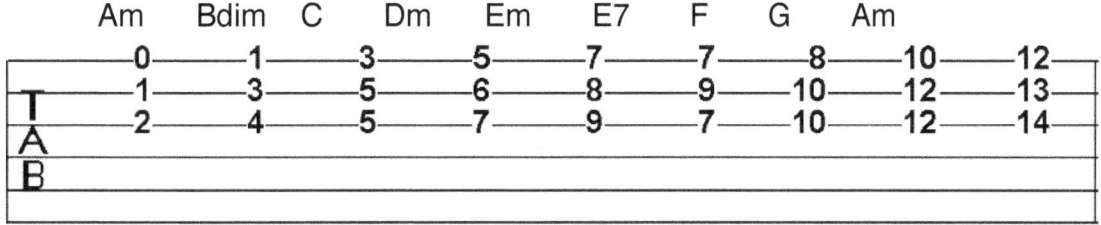

Local Major I-IV-V7 Chords, Strings 123

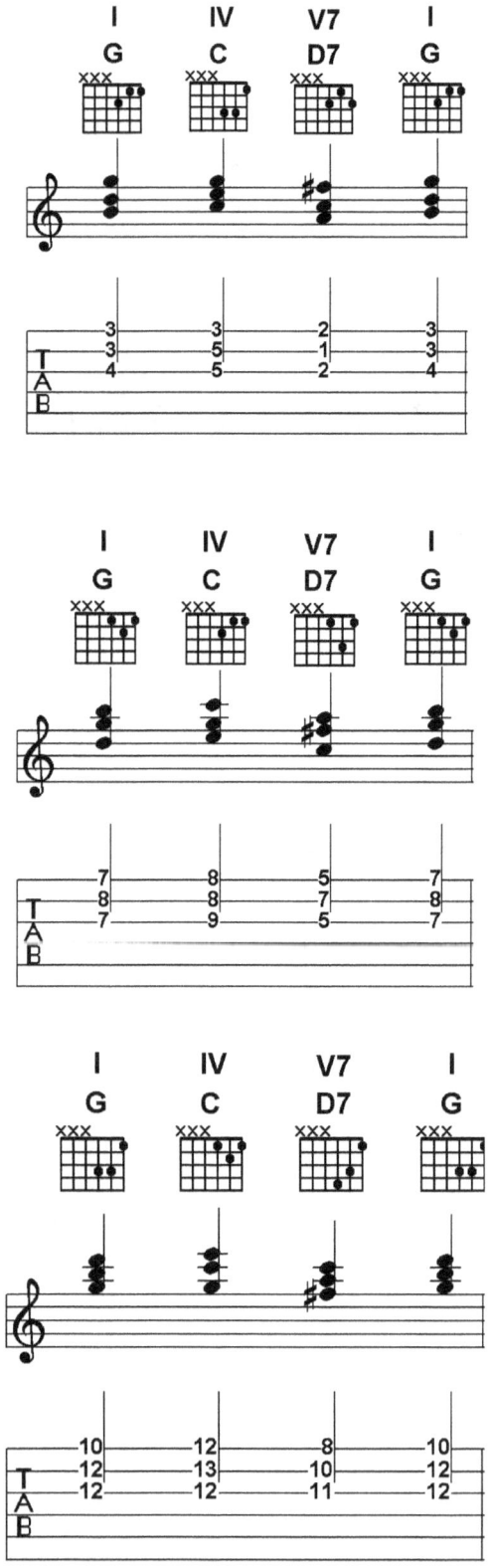

Local Minor i-iv-V7 Chords, Strings 123

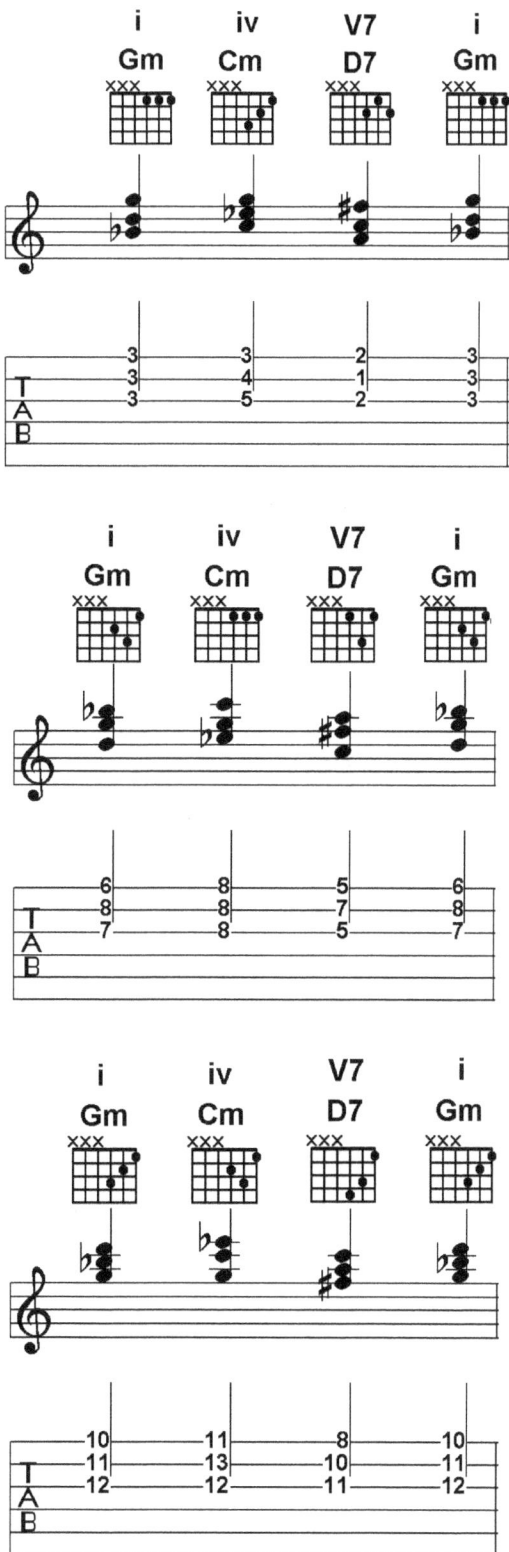

Triad Scales

Triad Scales use the nine shapes you just learned to create scales in a way that allows each chord tone to have its own string. With just nine shapes, you can create scales for the chord combinations that the chord progression is asking for. No matter where the chord progression goes—whether it is major, minor, or dominant seventh, whether it is in a major key or a minor key—you will have the right scale for just that situation with three chord tones and three passing tones.

Chord tones are golden because they are actually in the Chord. If you resolve (stop) on a note that just doesn't sound right, go to the next note in the scale in either direction.

In a nutshell, "**Triad Scales**" combine the nine shapes to make scales. At any given moment, you're only dealing with two of the shapes. When you get familiar with the shapes you will realize that, no matter where the chord progression goes, you will have a scale that fits that moment of the song and a picture that is easy to remember and easy to see and find.

The part that we care about is that we are going to make our scales by taking one shape with three notes in it and combining it with another shape that has three notes in it.

Making Scales with Chords

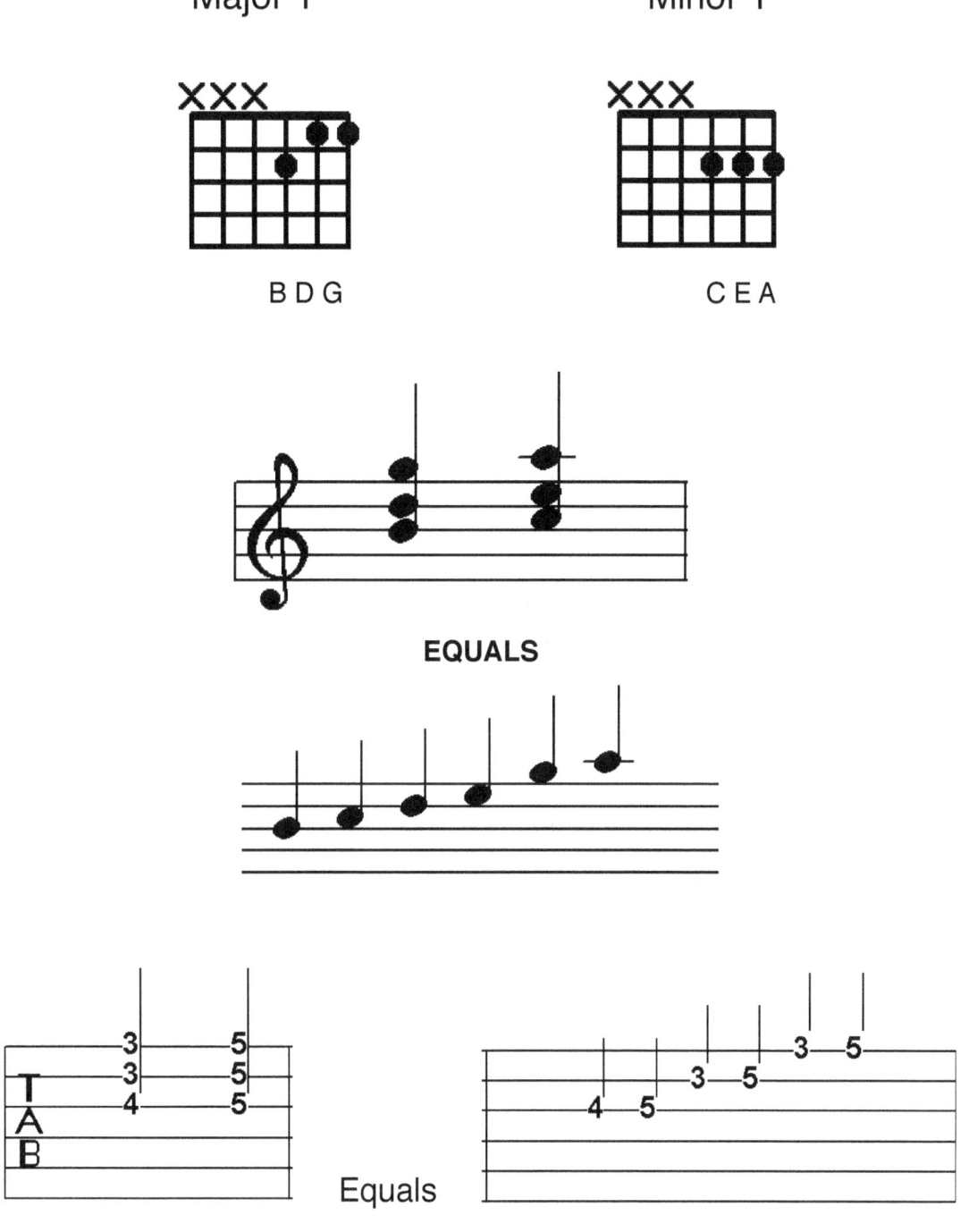

The Triad Scale

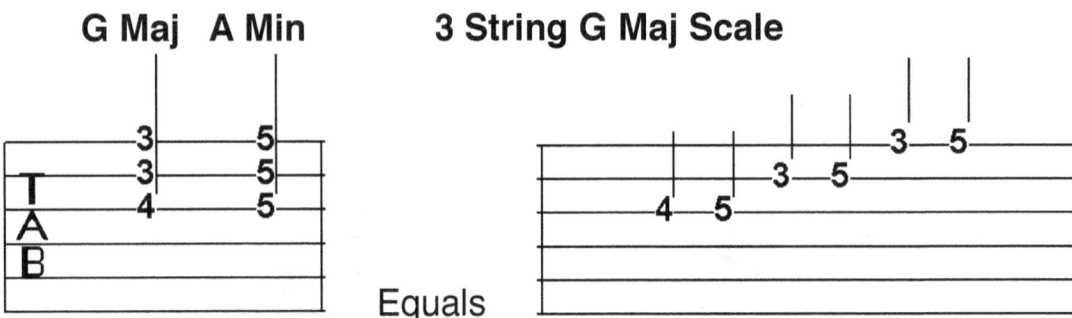

Since we are combining chords to make scales, I will write the scales in tab as two chords.

Above is the tablature for a G major triad and an A minor triad. On the right is the *Triad Scale* that it creates.

Just as the shapes help us have a picture of what we are dealing with, I believe that writing the chords to represent the scales (above) presents the chordal information, and the tab for the scale, in a picture (shape).

It is a quick, easy way to refer to the chords and give you the tablature for the scales.

Example Triad Scales, Strings 123

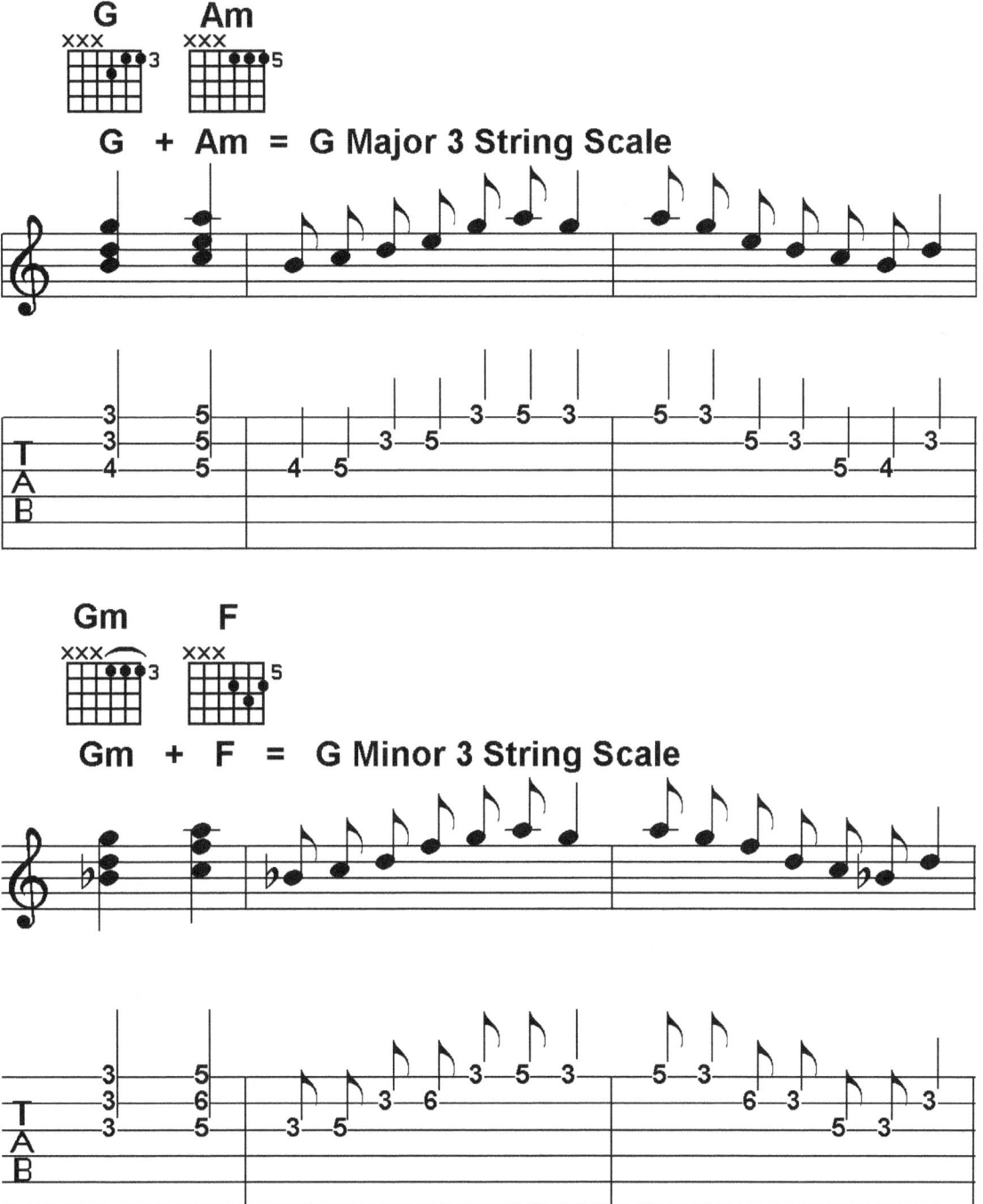

Major Triad Scales, Strings 123

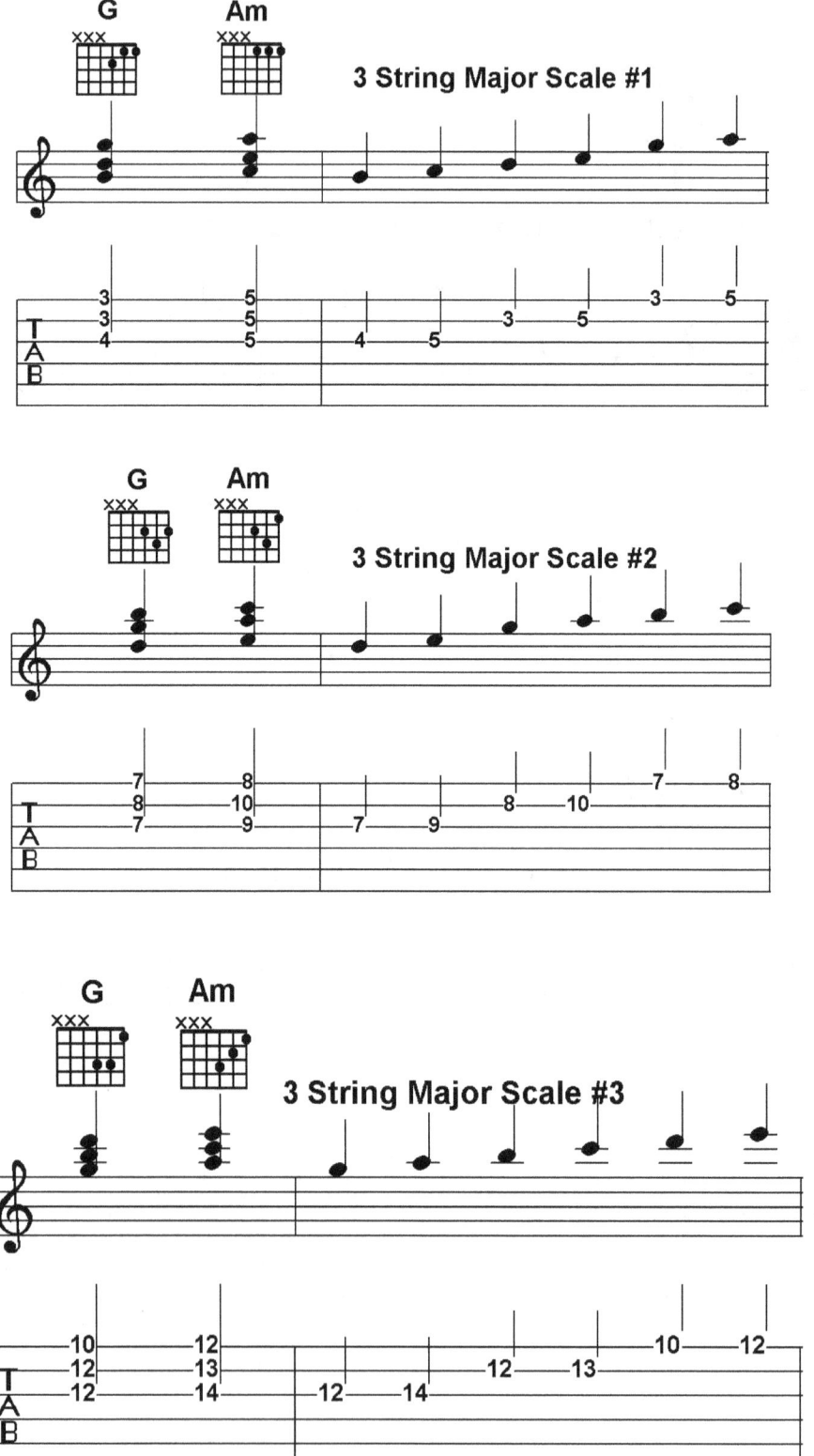

Minor Triad Scales, Strings 123

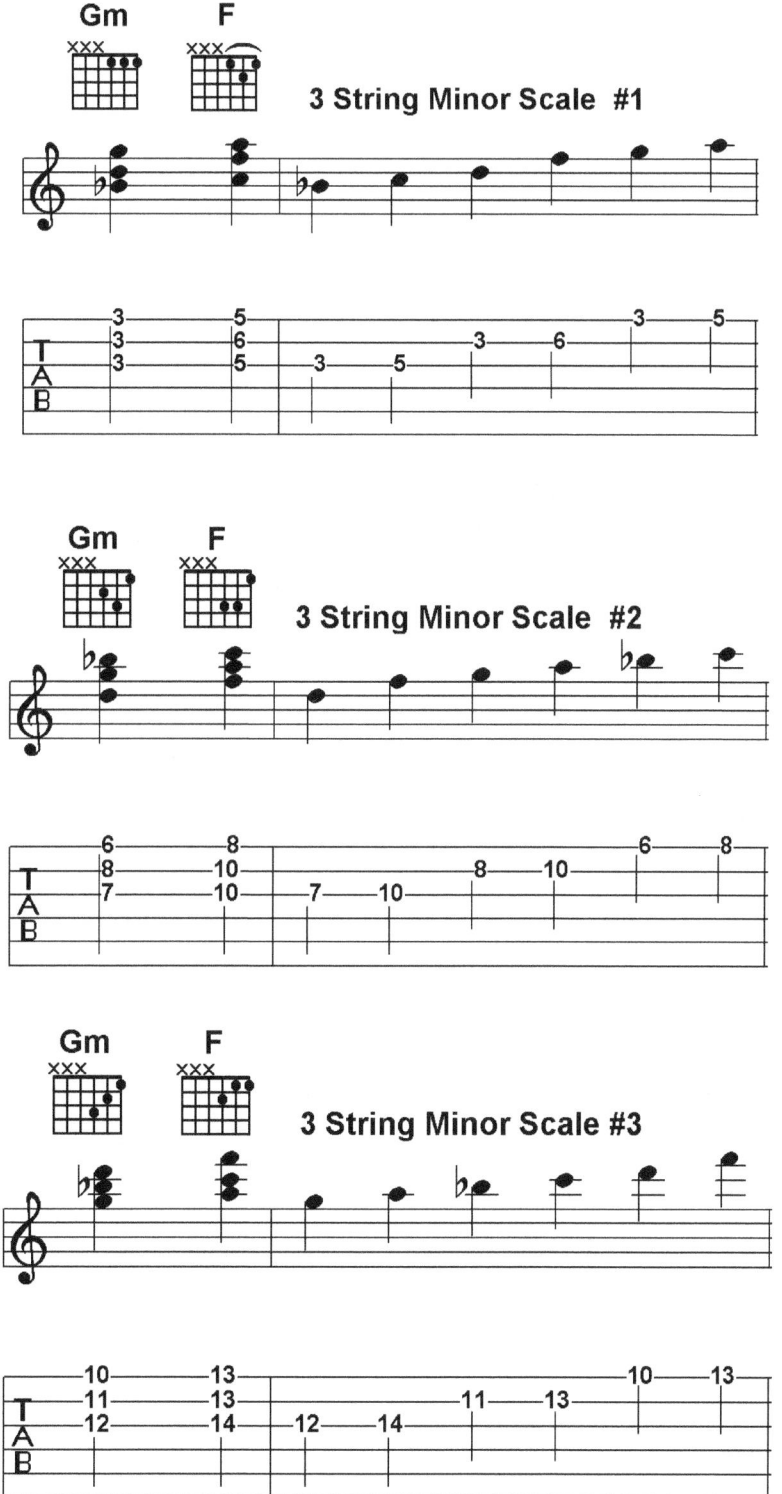

Major Key 7th Triad Scales, Strings 123

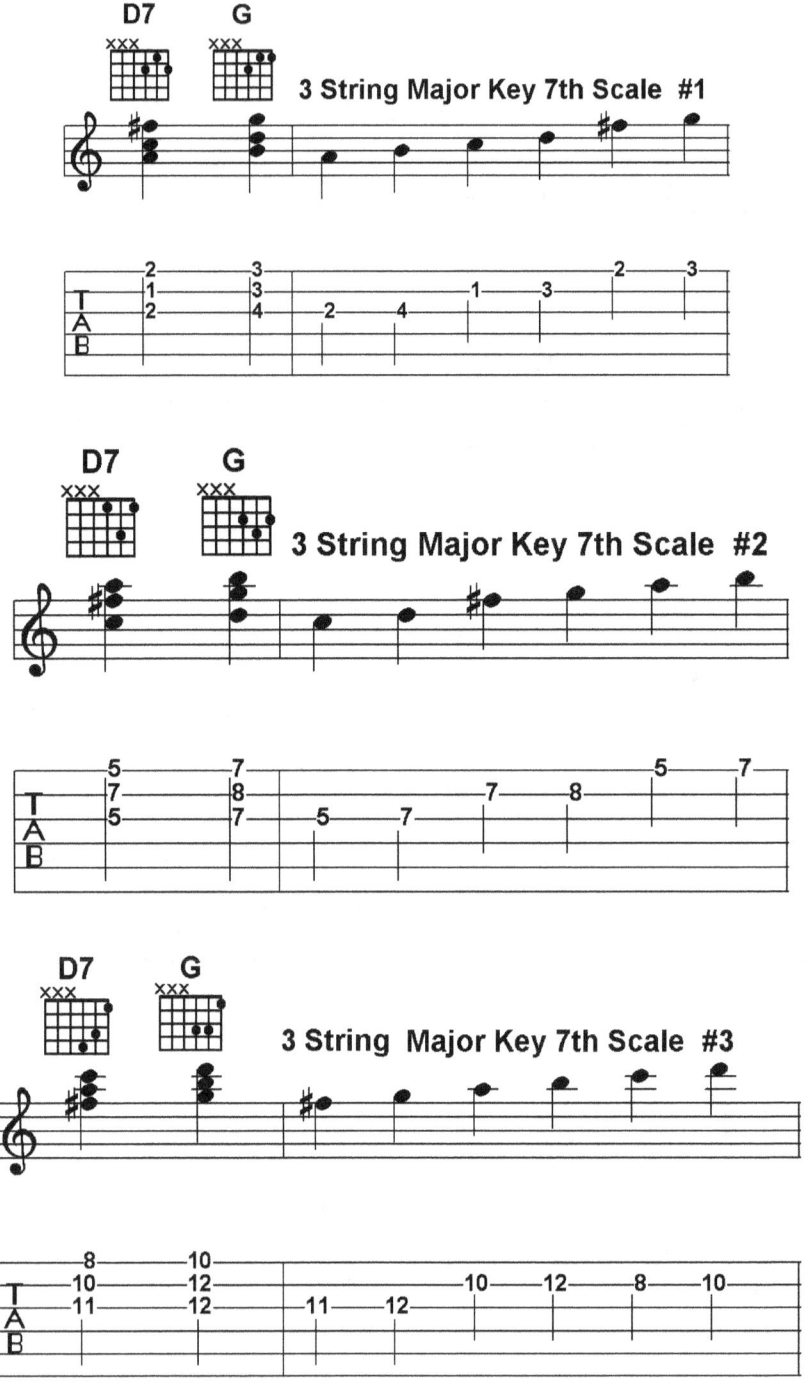

Minor Key 7th Triad Scales, Strings 123

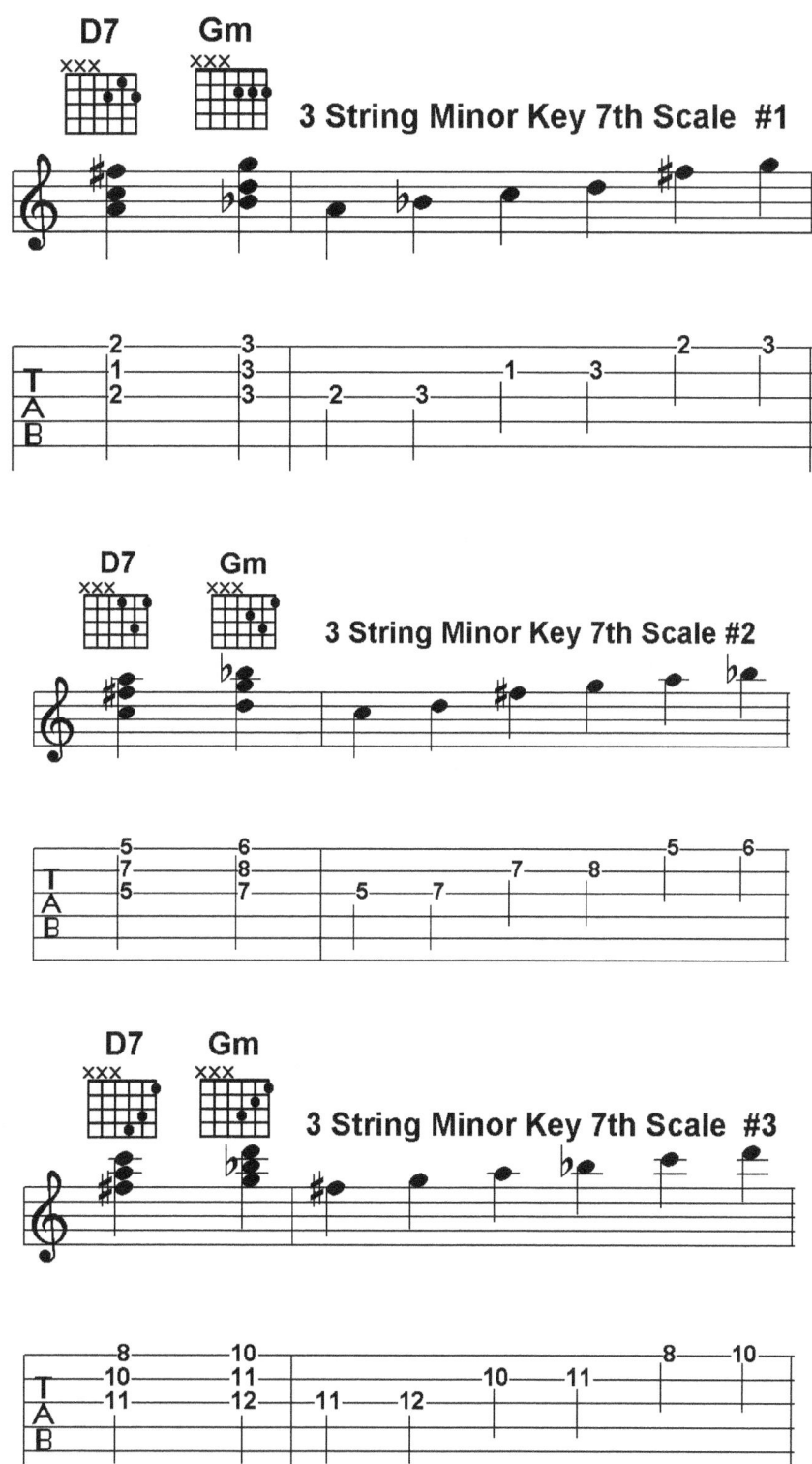

Local Major Key, Strings 123, #1
Root on String 1
Movable

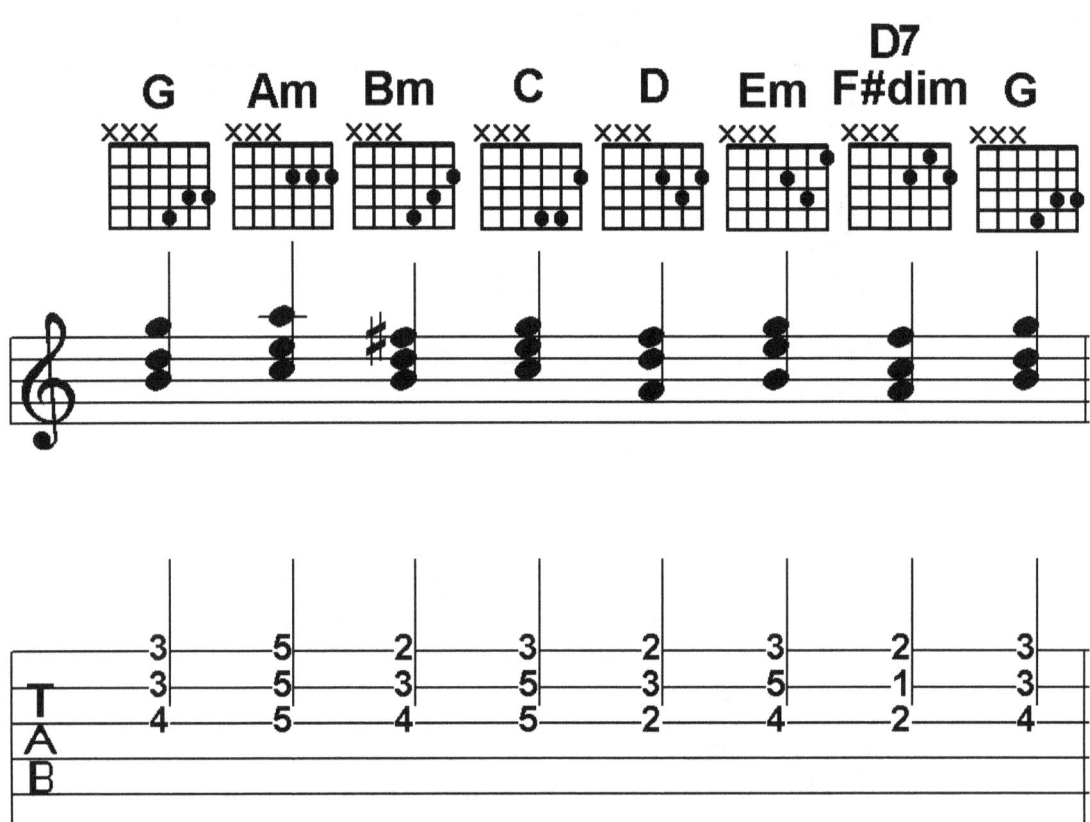

Local Major Key, Strings 123, #2
Root on String 2
Movable

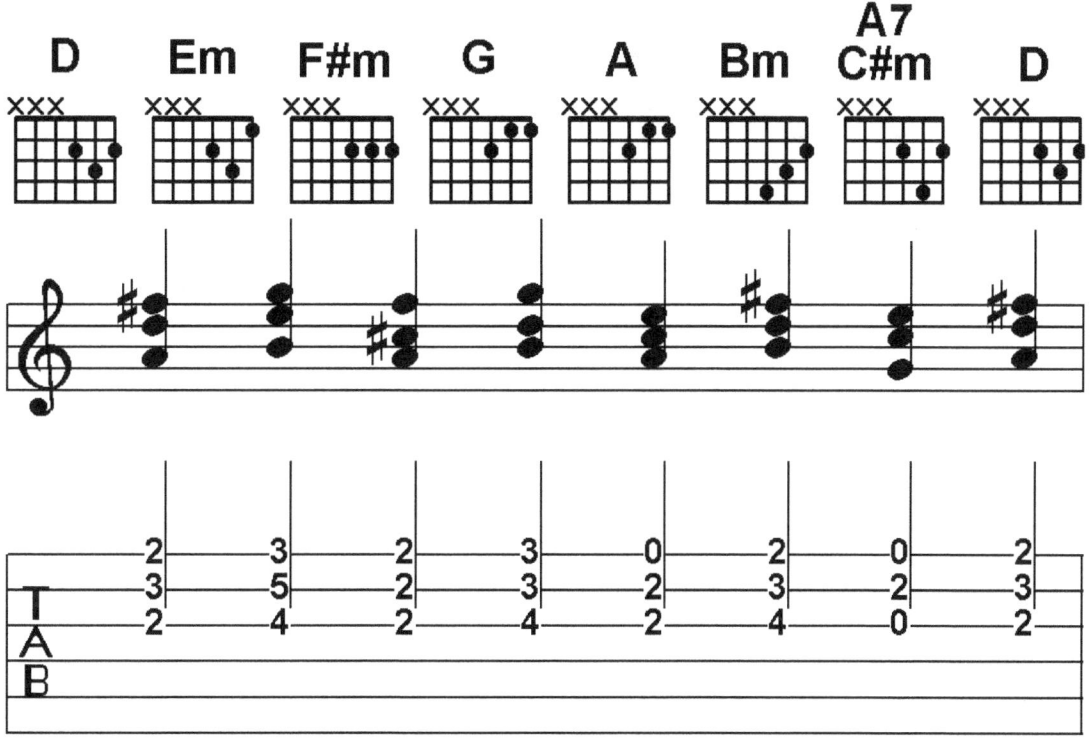

Local Major Key, Strings 123, #3
Root on String 3
Movable

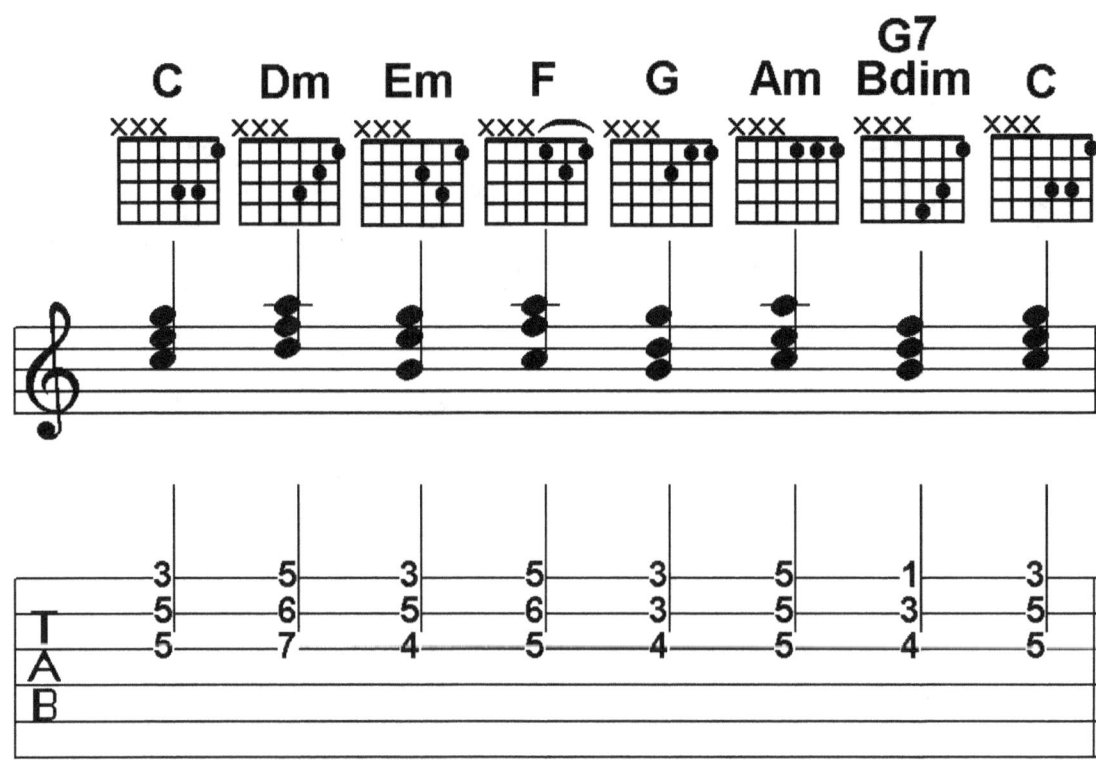

Local Major Keys, Strings 123

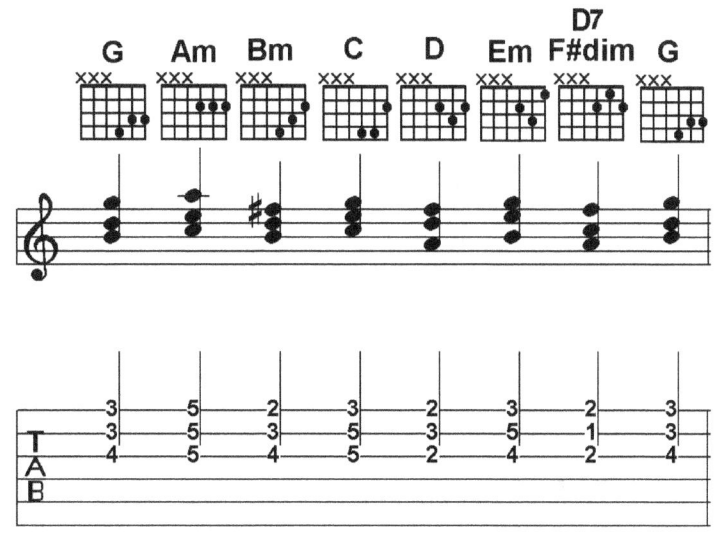

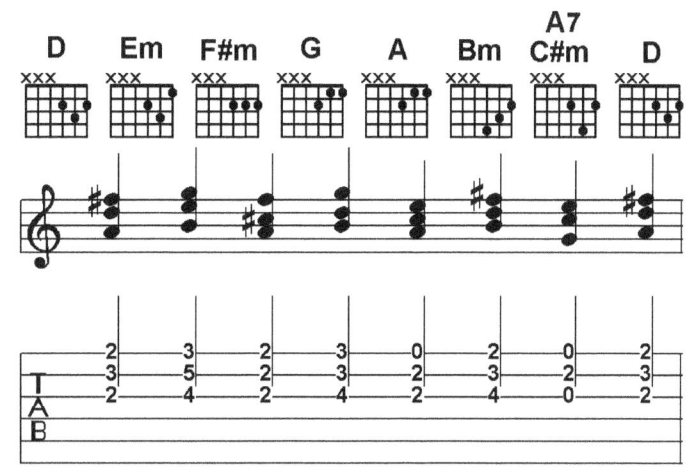

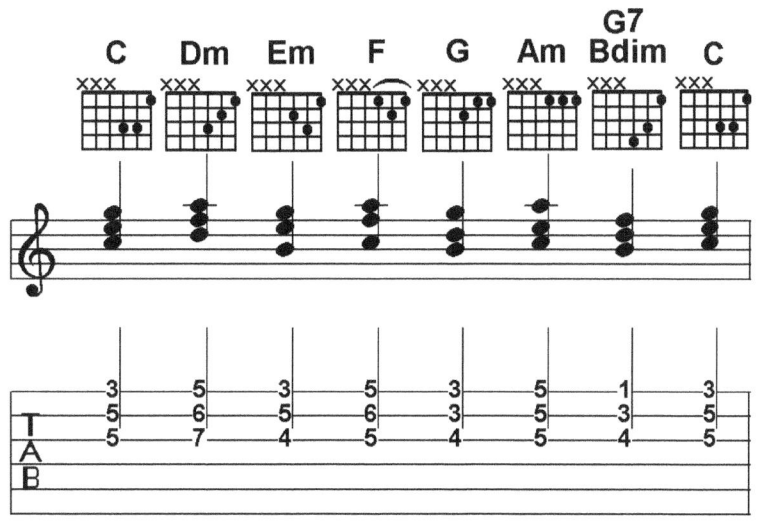

Neckology
Movable Chords

I don't know if the best thing about this next page is that it shows me every triad that is in the key of G major on strings 1, 2, and 3... or if it's that it's movable.

By movable, I mean that you can access all of the keys by moving your location on the neck. If you moved all of the triads in the key of G up one fret, you would have all the triads in the key of G#. If you moved all of the triads in the key of G# up one fret, you would have all the triads in the key of A. And so on.

Local G Major Key, Strings 123

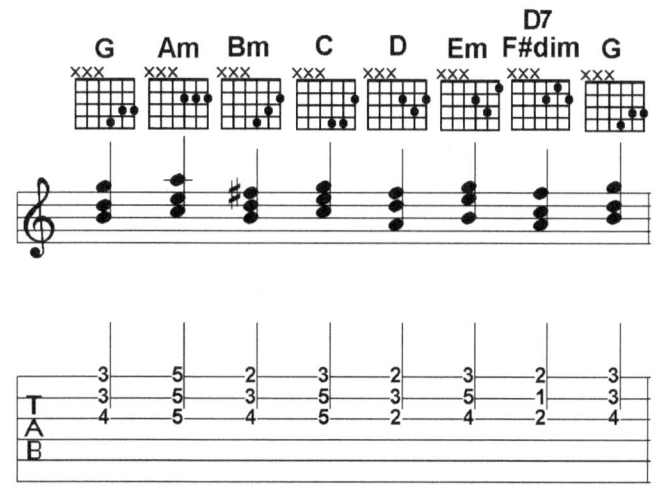

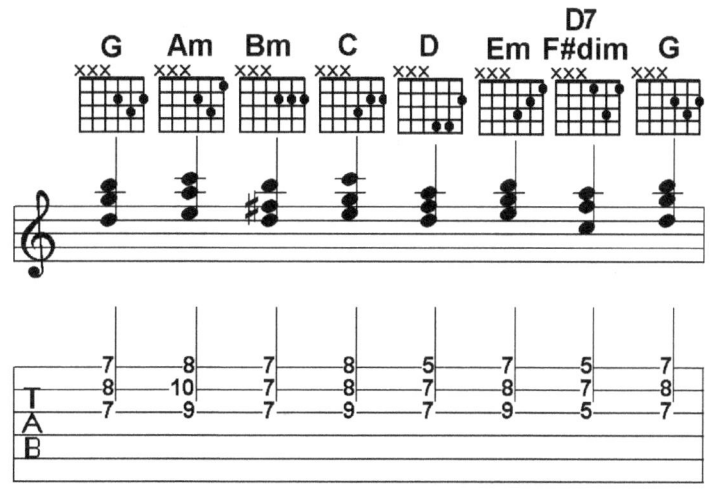

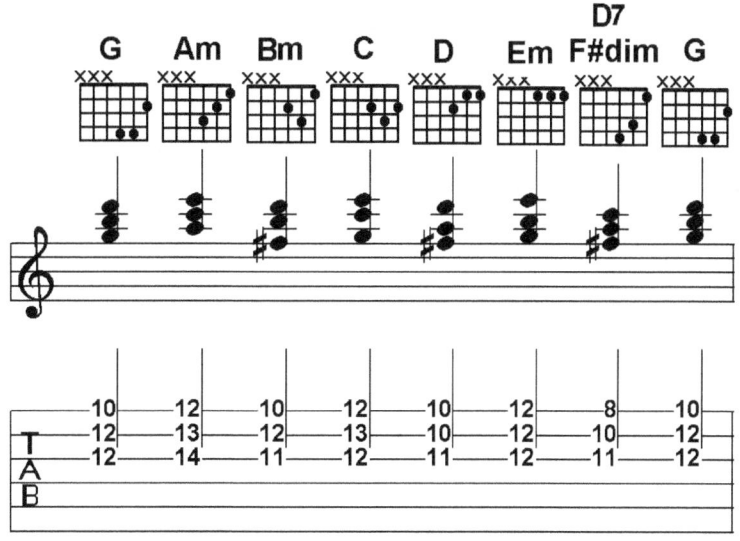

The 6 String Triad Scales

The 6 String Scales have 12 notes in each group; 6 are chord tones, and 6 are passing tones. Each string has a chord tone and a passing tone. It is symmetrical and it is movable.

They are made up of two adjacent triads. One of the triads will display the chord tones and the other will display the passing tones.

If you know your triads you can use them to create custom scales to play across any chord progression. The 6 String Scale *is organized to accommodate a single line melody (one note at a time).* The 3 String Scales *are for single line melody or harmonized leads à la Jimi Hendrix.*

We are going to deal with three kinds of scales: Major scales, Minor scales, and 7th scales.

There will be three locations for *Major* scales, one with the root on string 1, one with the root on string 2, and one with the root on string 3.

There will be three locations for *Minor* scales, one with the root on string 1, one with the root on string 2, and one with the root on string 3. There will be three locations for 7th scales for the Major keys and there will be three locations for 7th scales for the Minor keys.

6 String Triad Scales

6 String A Major Scale #1

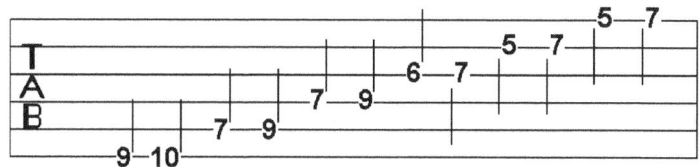

6 String A major Scale #2

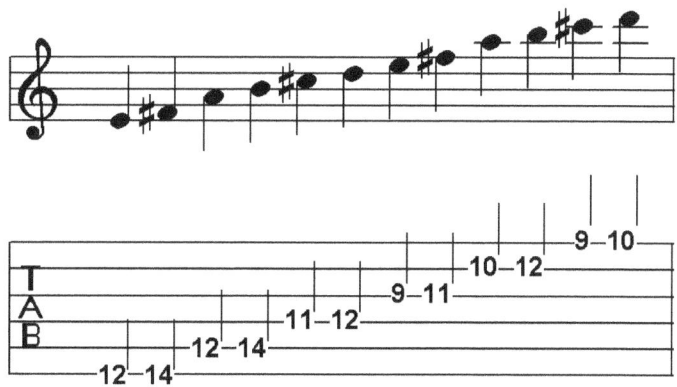

6 String A Major Scale #3

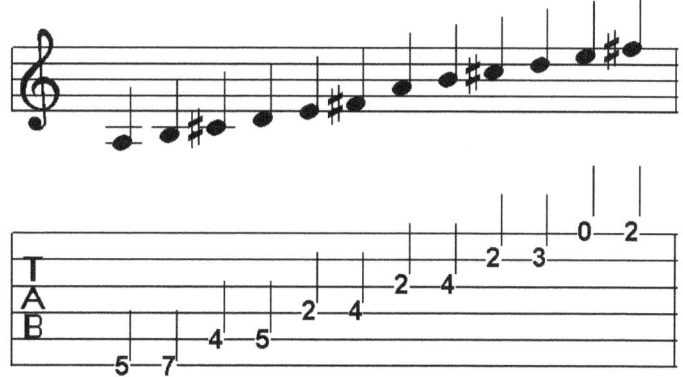

6 String Triad Scales

6 String A Minor Scale #1

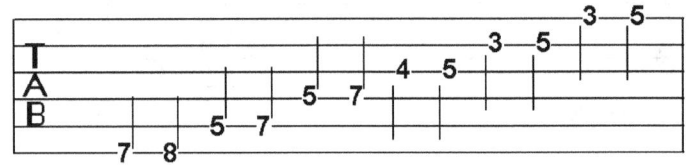

6 String A Minor Scale #2

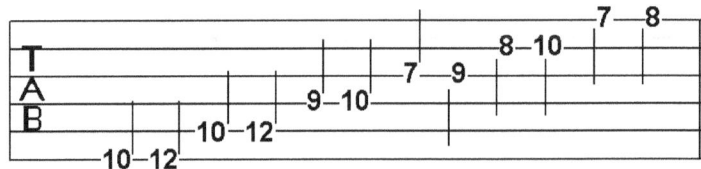

6 String A Minor Scale #3

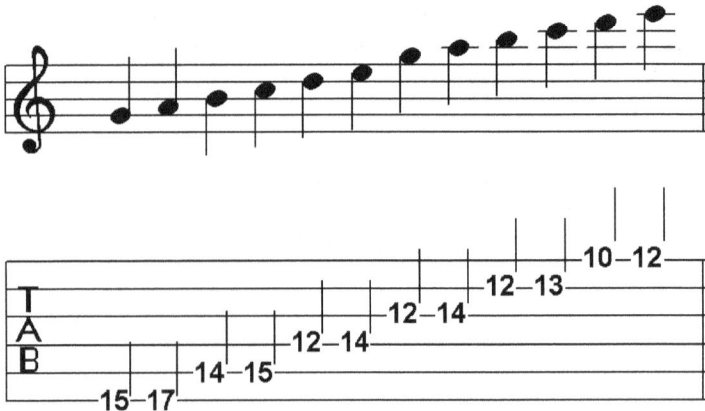

E7 6 String Triad Scales, Major Key

6 String 7th scale #1   Major Key

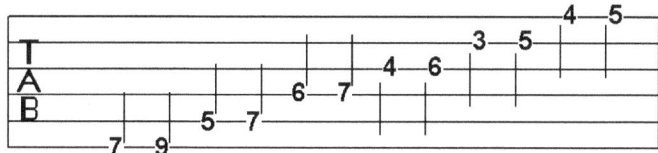

6 String 7th Scale #2 Major Key

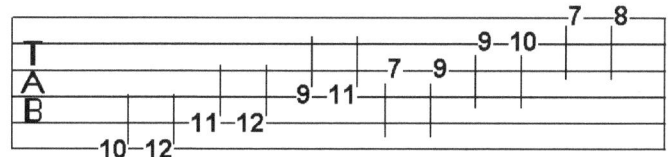

6 String 7th Scale #3   Major Key

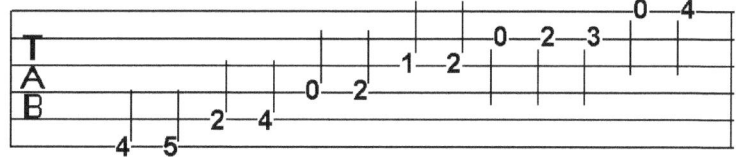

E7 6 String Triad Scales, Minor Key

6 String 7th Scale #1   Minor Key

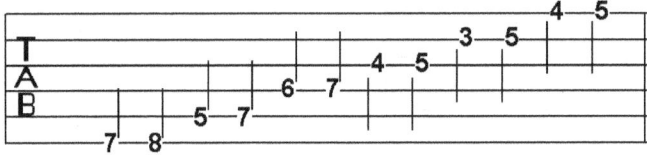

6 String E7th Scale #2 Minor Key

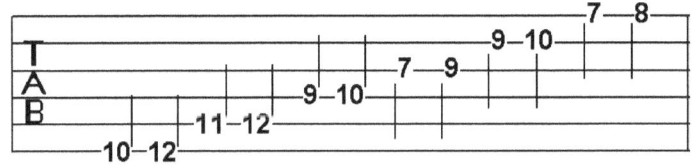

6 String 7th Scale #3 Minor Key

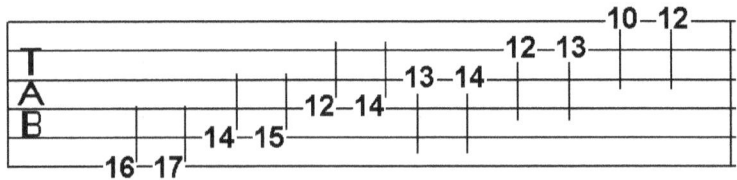

All 27 Triad Inversions

G Major

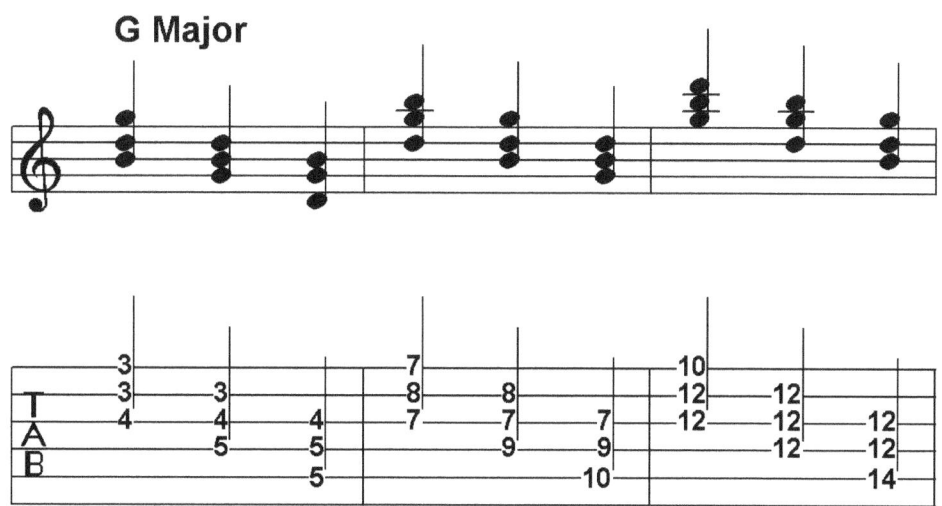

G Minor

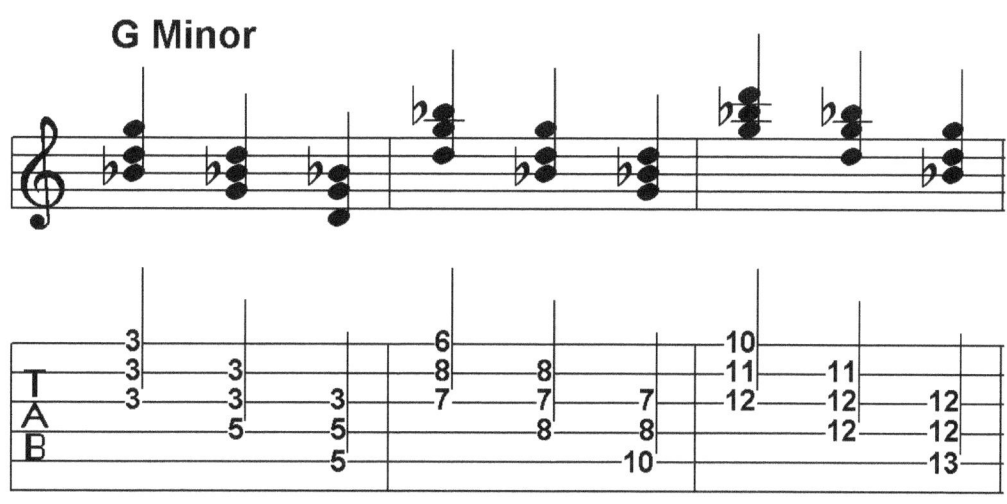

D7th

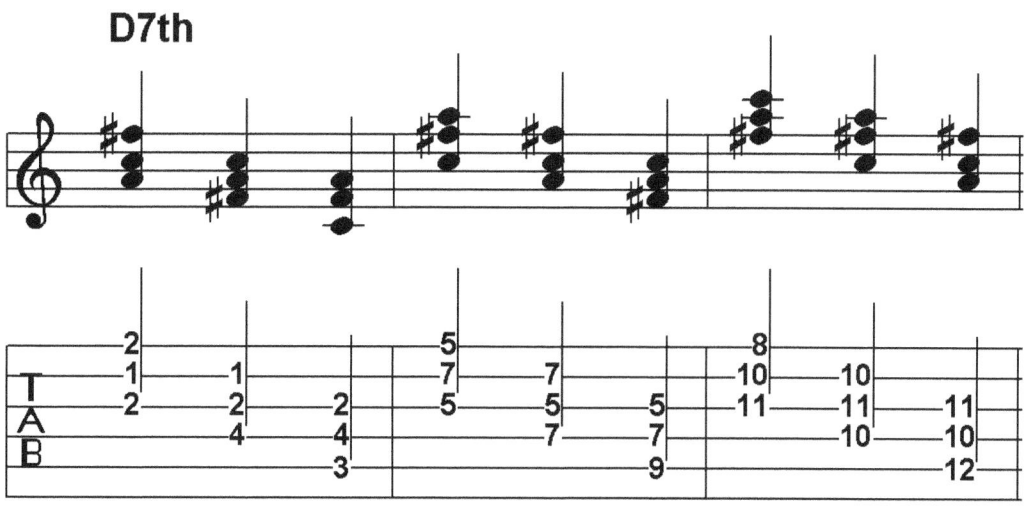